The DCC Survival Guide

Succeeding at the Army's Direct Commission Course

Garrett Ham

Becoming an Army JAG Officer: Book 1

Copyright © 2014 Garrett Ham

All rights reserved.

The views and opinions expressed in this book are the author's own and do not reflect the official policy or position of the United States Army, the National Guard Bureau, the Arkansas National Guard, the Department of Defense, or the United States Government.

ISBN: 1503083063
ISBN-13: 978-1503083066

DEDICATION

To my wife, who played single mother to two small children during my absence.

CONTENTS

Preface	1
DCC: Week 1	5
DCC: Week 2	11
DCC: Week 3	17
DCC: Week 4	23
DCC: Week 5	29
DCC: Week 6	35
DCC: Final Thoughts	39
Conclusion	47

PREFACE

The mystique surrounding the JAG Corps has permeated popular culture for years. Media depictions of the military attorney—from the dramatic courtroom maneuvers of Tom Cruise in *A Few Good Men* to the campy depictions of military justice in the television show *JAG*—have further compounded the public fascination with military law and order. The large number of applications that the Army receives every year from aspiring judge advocates further evidences the high level of interest this career field garners.

Upon becoming a JAG officer in March 2013, I found that, while I was able to find an abundance of material about the JAG Corps itself, I could find very little about the initial training process every new judge advocate must undergo. The Army's complete reformatting of the training program in 2013 made it nearly impossible to find accurate, up-to-date information. With my report date for the Direct Commission Course quickly approaching, I found myself wanting for information to help me prepare for the experience that lay before me. So, disappointed by the scarcity of material available, I decided to keep a weekly journal of my experiences to share with future JAG officers. If you have purchased this book, I suspect you fit this description, and I therefore hope that my work will help you begin training better prepared than I was.

This short volume is intended to serve as a quick reference guide for both those preparing for and those already undergoing Army JAG training. I am currently working on a more expansive volume that provides much greater detail about my experience and a more expanded exposition of my thoughts and advice regarding the process. This shorter volume, however, is meant to serve those who need a quick reference to understand their training obligations. Consequently, I have divided this book into brief week-by-week chapters, which are further segregated into a description of my experiences and my tips to remember as you undergo your own training.

Be aware that the Army is always tinkering with its training processes, so it is likely that your experience will differ somewhat from my own.

About Me

I currently serve as a JAG officer in the National Guard, meaning that I serve part-time—one weekend per month, two weeks per year. This book, however, is meant to provide guidance to every Army JAG officer, whether active duty, Reserve, or National Guard. Since all JAG officers attend the same initial training and must meet the same standards, there is no need to draw distinctions between the different components in this volume.

The National Guard and Army Reserve, however, are unique in that their judge advocates usually begin drilling upon commissioning, rather than waiting until the completion of their initial entry training. Since a significant wait between commissioning and commencement of training is not unusual, Reserve and National Guard officers are often able to gain substantial experience prior to the beginning of training. If your DCC report date is your first day in the Army—which is generally the case for active duty judge advocates—you may want to seek out one of these officers, as he or she will likely have a better grasp of what's going on. (Of course, prior service officers are almost always the best resource.)

JAG Training

All new judge advocates must attend two phases of training. The first phase—and subject of this volume—is the Army's Direct Commission Course located at Fort Benning, Georgia. This six-week course teaches basic soldiering skills, such as land navigation, marksmanship, and the customs and courtesies of the Army. Even officers with prior commissioned service must complete this course, so you will probably have West Point, ROTC, and OCS graduates in your class.

After completing DCC, you will move on to the second phase of training: the Judge Advocate Officer Basic Course (JAOBC) in Charlottesville, Virginia. This eleven-week course is a more academic, classroom experience focusing on the unique aspects of military law.

As I mentioned earlier, this structure marks a significant departure from the previous training regiment. Prior to July 2013, new judge advocates spent their first two weeks in-processing into the Army at Fort Lee, Virginia, then completed JAOBC before concluding at DCC, so even fairly recent resources are already out of date.

I would be remiss if I failed to mention those officers attending the Direct Commission Course who are not judge advocates. The Army allows a small number of officers in fields other than law, chaplaincy, and medicine to receive a direct commission, though this is often reserved for experienced enlisted personnel. Only two members of my class fit this description—they were easy to identify by their second lieutenant rank—but the number of these officers will vary from class to class. I have decided to release these JAG training guides in two installments to recognize these officers who may benefit from this *DCC Survival Guide* but who will have little use for my advice regarding the JAG School.

DCC: WEEK 1

The Army's Direct Commission Course teaches basic soldiering skills to direct commission officers. A direct commission officer is an officer who receives a commission without first completing a commissioning program through West Point, ROTC, or OCS. Direct commissions are normally reserved for professionals who serve a very particular function within the Army—such as doctors, chaplains, and lawyers.

This means that everyone attending DCC is a commissioned officer. So, unlike the traditional commissioning routes, the purpose of this course is not to provide a means to earn a commission; everyone is already commissioned. Rather, DCC trains commissioned officers to act appropriately in the United States Army.

Noncommissioned officers—that is, enlisted personnel in the rank of corporal and above—primarily lead the course, though there are a few officers who provide instruction from time to time. While NCOs have traditionally served as the primary instructors in officer candidate courses in every branch but the Air Force, DCC is unique because the students are already officers. This means that the students technically outrank the teachers.

This creates an interesting atmosphere. The stereotypical military training environment characterized by loud yelling and flamboyant reprimands is largely absent from DCC. The enlisted leadership still provides instruction and corrects mistakes—sometimes forcefully—but the unique structure of the course becomes apparent the first time you hear "sir" or "ma'am" follow a chewing out.

The quality of your NCOs will vary. My class had some really good ones and some pretty mediocre ones. If you want to learn the material, however, you should be able to do so, though you may have to take the initiative if your instructors are subpar. You received a direct commission because the Army believes you to be a highly-qualified professional. You are therefore expected to take responsibility for your own instruction.

The presence of students with prior experience as commissioned officers forms another interesting aspect of the class. Even though the course is designed to teach basic officership, the Army recently decided to require *all* entrants to the JAG Corps to attend the Direct Commission Course. Consequently, my class had a handful of captains and prior classes have even had majors. Given the condensed nature of the course—ROTC and West Point are four-year programs and OCS is a twelve-week course that follows nine weeks of basic training—the Army believes having experience in the ranks helps the new officers acclimate to Army standards quickly. So, in a sense, these officers serve more as instructors than trainees.

Fort Benning

DCC is conducted entirely on the grounds of Fort Benning, Georgia. Fort Benning is a very big post, housing a large number of units and schools. The Army's Armor School, Infantry School, Airborne School, Officer Candidate School, NCO Academy, and Infantry Basic Training are all conducted there. In addition, elements of the 75th

Ranger Regiment have a presence there as well.

Fort Benning has a storied history and enjoyed renewed fame with the 2002 release of *We Were Soldiers*, which was largely filmed on the post. If you have seen the film, you will recognize much of the scenery from the movie. The officer housing and the airborne towers are particularly identifiable.

As far as the actual DCC lodgings, our barracks were much nicer than I expected. While not luxurious in any sense of the word, each room housed only two officers and had its own bathroom. This made the accommodations quite nice by Army standards. Of course, you will spend very little time in your room, but the arrangements make it much easier to take a shower in the mornings. So, DCC is *not* basic training. There are no open-bay barracks or community showers.

Week 1 Training

The first week of military training is often the most difficult because of the anxiety associated with starting a new program. You do not need to be anxious about the first week of DCC, which is devoted mostly to in-processing. You will wait in a lot of lines and fill out a lot of repetitive paperwork. You will also receive basic classwork instruction on various topics of Army life, structure, and tradition and spend a significant amount of time learning drill and ceremony—marching, saluting, etc.

Note that it is likely you will spend the first week or so wearing your PT uniform. Since these uniforms do not bear rank insignia, those outside the course will likely assume you are a basic trainee. Just roll with it. Don't be the jerk who tries to dress down a drill sergeant for reprimanding you. You will look and act like a new private, and nobody likes a new officer with an entitled attitude.

Physical Training

The Army has a unique physical training program that consists of a lot of strange exercises. You will become familiar with them during the first week of training and become very proficient in them during morning PT, which is conducted every morning at 0500. (If you are not already familiar with military time, I recommend you become so prior to showing up for training.)

You will also likely conduct a 1-1-1, which is essentially a half Army Physical Fitness Test (APFT), requiring one minute of pushups, one minute of sit-ups, and a one-mile run. This serves as a gauge for determining your current level of physical fitness. If you need improvement, however, do not expect morning PT to get you there. Morning PT does a poor job of preparing soldiers for the APFT, and many of my classmates found themselves in worse shape at the end of the course than at the beginning. You will have to spend your own time getting into shape.

Concluding Thoughts

Starting in week one and continuing until the last day of the course, you will be assigned CQ—charge of quarters—shifts. There must always be at least two people on CQ during off duty times—1800 to 0600 every duty day and then twenty-four hours per day during weekends and holidays. The duty essentially requires manning the CQ desk, answering the phone, and performing a variety of mundane tasks, such as sweeping and mopping the barrack floors.

The frequency of your duty will depend on the size of your class. I performed CQ duties about once a week. Of course, after a long day of training, it is never fun to wake up in the middle of the night for a two-hour shift, particularly when you have to wake up early the next morning. (The 0000 to 0200 shift is the worst.) This, however, is part of the military experience.

Expect the first week to be extremely slow and excruciatingly boring. Enjoy the slow pace before things really pick up.

Quick Tips

• Seek out the advice of prior-service classmates.

• Don't pull rank. You haven't earned it, and nobody likes an entitled officer.

• Show up in good shape and exercise in your free time. Do not expect DCC to prepare you for the APFT.

DCC: WEEK 2

With in-processing (hopefully) complete, week two begins the "real" training. To get the week started, we spent about four hours at the Central Issue Facility (CIF) receiving the gear we would need during the course, including a ruck sack, body armor, a Kevlar helmet, and a variety of other items. You will also receive a large number of items that you will never use—but which CIF insists on giving you anyway—so be very careful not to lose anything; otherwise you'll find your pay docked.

Land Navigation

Even though it extends into the third week, the highlight of week two is land navigation. If you are a hunter or just like spending time outdoors, you will probably love this part of the course, as it allows you to spend large amounts of time in the woods. We devoted Thursday of this week to classroom instruction, where we learned how to plot points on a map and properly use a compass and pace distance.

On Friday, the cadre drove us to a large wooded area where they divided us into three-person teams and gave each team three points to find. We then had three hours to find them using only a map and compass. In the afternoon, the cadre gave us three more points.

Each point was marked with a small, numbered sign. When we reached a point, we had to write down the number on the sign to confirm that we had in fact found the correct one. This was important because, since there are several marked points in the area, we had no way of knowing if the point we found was actually our assigned point until we got back to the starting line. Occasionally, a previous good Samaritan had written the point's coordinates on the sign, but not all signs were marked—the cadre tend to replace marked signs when they discover them—and some were marked incorrectly. Consequently, you will be unable to verify if the point you find is in fact the point you are trying to find. Finding a small sign in the middle of the woods is not exceptionally easy, particularly when you consider that the dot you make on your map when plotting your points could itself represent about 100 square meters—everything is on the metric system—of actual space.

The ease with which you can veer from your original angle of approach while circumventing brush and other obstacles in the woods further complicates the effort. If you leave the road traveling at a 270 degree angle to your point and you readjust to that angle after moving around a tree, you can very easily end up several hundred meters from your goal by the time you cross the appropriate distance.

In addition, the difficulty of properly pacing your distance further compounds the challenge. You estimate the distance you travel by measuring how many steps it takes you to walk one hundred meters, which you estimate by walking a one-hundred-meter path before you start. This is not an exact science, particularly when you consider how the unstable terrain in the woods can alter your pacing.

If you are concerned about your ability to do this, I would simply say that I did well despite a horrible sense of direction—I even get lost in my hometown. Just be sure to listen carefully to the instructors and the prior service officers.

Some Details of Army Life

This is a good time to mention some of the eccentricities of Army training. Uniformity is heavily stressed in the Army to the point of defying logic and common sense. This is simply part of it, and so I recommend embracing it. I believe a brief anecdote from my class's experience during land navigation illustrates this point well.

The first morning we went out, temperatures were below freezing and the wind chill was about seventeen degrees. We were all issued Gore-Tex jackets for the course. These jackets have a flap on the chest on which to place the rank insignia. Unfortunately, however, the PX did not have seventy first lieutenant rank sleeves, and so not everyone was able to purchase one prior to our first day of land navigation. Since we did not all have the rank sleeve, no one could wear the jackets in formation.

This might not sound like a big deal, but you will quickly realize that you spend a very large amount of time in formation waiting to receive the necessary briefings and for the cadre to prepare. It is not unusual to stand in formation for more than an hour at a time. So we all stood out there in seventeen-degree weather with no jackets. One of my classmates was treated for frostbite that day. Whether she would have gotten frostbite anyway I don't know, but I believe the point is clear. There are some things that the Army takes very seriously, no matter how ridiculous they may seem. If you go into training accepting that this is just the way things are, you'll do much better than those who insist on constantly vocalizing their opinions.

Further compounding the absurdity of that morning were the heat-safety procedures. Procedure is everything in the Army, and safety regulations require that a heat exhaustion station—which included Gatorade and water dispensers and a cooler full of wet towels—be present during training events. So we had to set one up for a training event where a classmate was frostbitten. This is simply part of being in the Army.

I reiterate this point to emphasize the importance of accepting there is nothing you can do to change this, and so you should simply accept it. There are a lot of things you will have to do that you think are stupid, but you do them anyway. Keep a sense of humor about it, and you should do fine. Maybe when you wear a star on your chest you can do something about it, but in the meantime, learn to keep a good attitude.

Other Second Week Activities

We spent the rest of week two focused on a variety of smaller, less memorable tasks. This week contained a particularly large amount of classroom instruction, the most significant being a course on battlefield first-aid. This was an interesting class, though the bulk of the instruction centered around properly applying a tourniquet. Since most preventable battlefield deaths occur as a result of blood loss, first-aid focuses on stopping bleeding until the casualty can be evacuated to an aid station.

Other classroom instruction included a lecture on military legal history and resiliency training, which is a training program the Army implemented in response to the rise of suicide rates among soldiers during the previous decade of war. Resiliency training sessions focus primarily on handling stress and dealing with anger and depression, and we took several of these courses during our time at DCC.

Physical training during week two was pretty light. We conducted a two-mile ruck march, which essentially means we walked two miles in our ACUs with a large backpack full of gear. Since you must perform a six-mile ruck march in less than one hour and forty-eight minutes to graduate, these shorter ruck marches—you will also perform a four-mile ruck march during the course—prepare you to meet that requirement.

One interesting aspect of the second week occurred on Saturday. While weekends during DCC are normally free, on this Saturday we all went to the National Infantry Museum located outside the gates of Fort Benning. The museum traces the various conflicts of the United States with particular focus on the infantry. Since Fort Benning is the home of the infantry, the exhibits also tend to connect history to Fort Benning. Armor has recently moved to Fort Benning from Fort Knox, Kentucky, so a cavalry and armor museum is scheduled to open nearby sometime in the next few years.

There is also an IMAX in the museum. Most of the shows are educational programs—such as National Geographic documentaries—but it occasionally does show mainstream movies.

The second week of DCC was a busy but enjoyable one. After the monotony of the first week, week two provides you the opportunity to actually train.

Quick Tips

• Land navigation is not an insurmountable challenge, even if you have a horrible sense of direction. Listen to the cadre, and you'll do fine.
• A lot of what you have to do may seem stupid and ridiculous. Just roll with it and don't complain. These experiences often make for good stories later.

DCC: WEEK 3

During week three, the land navigation coursework that formed the thrust of week two's instruction comes to final fruition with the testing of your skills on the Red Diamond Land Navigation Course. You must demonstrate a basic level of competence in land navigation to pass DCC, but don't worry, everyone in my class passed.

Finishing Land Navigation

We began Monday of week three with another practice round. This time we divided into groups of two and went to the course where we would actually test.

On Monday morning, my partner and I were given three hours to find four points. The Army requires that you be tested in both daytime and nighttime conditions. Rather than conduct two separate tests, we began about an hour before sunrise, so that we performed both daytime and nighttime land navigation during the same event. After plotting our points, my partner and I had to walk a few kilometers down the road to get to where we needed to enter the woods. By the time we plotted our points and made this walk, there was enough light to allow us to trek through the woods fairly comfortably. (Finding your way through the woods, and, in particular, trying to find small points, can be quite difficult in the dark.)

When we finished our first practice round, we returned to the starting point to enjoy an MRE (Meal Ready to Eat) for lunch before receiving another four points to find in the afternoon. Some of the points were relatively easy to find while others were surrounded by thick brush, making them very difficult to see. The difficulty of finding the points will largely depend on the time of the year you conduct your training. I tested in January, after the leaves and greenery had died and fallen away, so there was less brush to obscure my view. If you test during the summer, when everything is overgrown, you will probably have a much more difficult time than I did. You will also have to look out for snakes and other dangerous wildlife not active during the winter—although wild boars are present year-round.

Unlike the first land navigation course on which we practiced, the roads of Red Diamond are made of sand. Walking between ten and fifteen miles through sand in combat boots can be quite taxing. In fact, the best exercise I had during DCC were these miles I walked on the Red Diamond Course.

Because of the excessive amount of walking you will do, it is important to take precautions to minimize the blisters you develop on your feet. Breaking in your combat boots prior to DCC will go a long way. I also recommend wearing thin dress socks under your regular socks and putting moleskin on any pressure points you may have on your feet. These precautions may not completely prevent the development of blisters, but they will alleviate your discomfort.

While blisters may not sound like a big deal, I assure you that they can be and that you should take preventative measures. One of my classmates failed her first land navigation test because her blisters had become so severe she was simply unable to finish. In fact, she looked like she had leprosy and was put on medical profile for several days. So a little care on the front-end can increase your chance of success.

After our practice rounds on Monday, we returned to the land navigation course again on Tuesday. In the morning, we were supposed to have a chance to run the course alone before taking our test on Wednesday. Inclement weather was moving in quickly, however, so the cadre eliminated this practice round and moved the test to Tuesday morning. So, it is likely that you will have one more practice round than I did.

For the test, we were given four hours to find five points. Finding three out of five constituted a passing grade, but we had to find them alone without any assistance. This is taken very seriously, so you will find yourself in serious trouble if the cadre catches you speaking with anyone on the course.

In all, you should expect to start at about 0600 and finish at about 1000. (You will make it out to the course by 0500 or so to receive your briefing and to eat an MRE for breakfast.) If you are not back at the starting point when time runs out, you fail, no matter how many points you find.

You will notice that everyone has a different assignment of points, and the assignments are not exactly fair. Some people will be assigned five points that are all several kilometers away from each other, while others will have all their points close enough to finish the course within an hour. Most people fall somewhere in between.

The vast majority of my class passed on the first try. Those who failed were given two more opportunities, and everyone passed by the end of the course. If you are unable to pass land navigation by the end of training you will not graduate, but you will have one year to complete the requirement with your home unit. If you do so, you will receive your diploma in the mail. If you do not pass within a year, however, you will likely lose your commission and be discharged, so it is something that you should take very seriously.

Other Week Three Activities

The unusual winter weather created a unique experience for my class. You may recall January 2014 news reports depicting the city of Atlanta at a standstill on account of a few inches of snowfall. Pictures of traffic gridlock in the city received a lot of airtime. It was only about three inches of snow, but, since it is so rare in Georgia, the state lacked the infrastructure to deal with it.

So, as a result of the weather, we were released early on Tuesday, and the post was shut down on Wednesday. While it was nice to have the day off, with the entire post shut down, there really wasn't anything to do. The cadre issued us MREs because the cafeteria and all the restaurants on post were closed.

Training finally resumed at noon on Thursday. We were originally scheduled to do some rappelling, but that was cancelled on account of construction in the area surrounding Thunderbolt Tower, so we devoted that Thursday to more resiliency training.

Basic Rifle Marksmanship

Friday finally got us back on track, as we began basic rifle marksmanship training. We were issued M16s, and we spent the morning in the classroom learning about the weapon and what we would have to do to qualify on it. We then spent the afternoon learning and practicing the correct firing positions. You do not get to choose from which positions you would like to fire; you must do it the Army way.

As a side note, you may use M4s instead of M16s. When I went through, DCC was one of the few pockets of the Army still using the M16. The M16s are much more difficult to fire, particularly for shorter individuals, as the M4s are shorter and lighter weight.

One interesting note about qualifying is the requirement to wear body armor. Whenever we used our weapons we had to be in full combat garb. This makes handling the weapon very awkward until you get used to it—and I don't think I ever really did. If I could do it over again, I would have spent time walking around in a weighted vest to get ready for the course.

Quick Tips

• Take good care of your feet. It will make a big difference in helping you succeed.
• Forget what you already know about firing a gun. You will have to learn to do things the Army way.

DCC: WEEK 4

The fourth week of DCC is almost completely devoted to basic rifle marksmanship. BRM consumes three weeks of enlisted basic training, so this week was a very condensed training regiment, leaving us little time for anything else.

A Week of Shooting

On Monday, we went to a computer simulator to get comfortable with the weapon. There we were given a mock M16 that plugged into a computer program and allowed us to shoot at targets on a large screen. It was like the old *Duck Hunt* game but on a much larger scale. I found this experience quite frustrating, as I could never hit anything and had a difficult time figuring out how the system worked. This was a problem for a lot of people, but others took right to it.

The next day we went to the zero range, where we zeroed in our scope. (For those not familiar with the process, zeroing in a scope involves shooting at paper targets twenty-five meters away and adjusting the scope until the red dot in the optic matches the bullet's trajectory.) The goal was to group three shots together on the target; it was not necessarily to get as close to the center as possible. So, I had a few rounds where I got all my shots very close to the center but not close enough to each other to be considered zeroed.

Breathing between shots inevitably moves your point of aim, and so I found it difficult to do what the cadre wanted. One of my classmates had what I thought to be the best approach. The cadre told us to breath in, exhale, and then shoot in that moment between the exhale and the next inhale—those who are experienced hunters are probably familiar with this approach. The problem with this, however, is that, with each breath, your weapon inevitably moves, forcing you to make small adjustments. So, to avoid this problem, one of my classmates fired three shots on one breath, squeezing off three rounds between one exhale and the next inhale. I would recommend trying this if you have any trouble.

Regardless of how quickly you zero, expect the process to take all day. Everything is done as a group, so you will have to wait for everyone to zero their scopes before you can leave. We spent all day at the range, and we only left because it was getting dark. When we left, there were still several people who had yet to zero their scopes.

On Wednesday, we went to the actual range where we would qualify. This range had targets shaped like soldiers that would pop up from behind berms at various distances ranging from fifty to three hundred meters. Those who were unable to zero their scopes, however, had to go back to the zero range to complete the process.

On Thursday, we did practice qualifications in the morning. To qualify, we had to hit twenty-three out of forty pop-up targets. Only one target would pop up at a time—except a few rounds where two would pop up—and we had a few seconds to adjust and fire. We only had enough ammunition to fire once at each target, so firing multiple times at one target was a good way to run out of ammunition before the test was complete. Still, if you miss an easy one, it may be a good idea to try again and then refrain from shooting a more difficult target later. The practice round is a good time for you to develop your own strategies for success.

You will have to shoot from three different positions to qualify: the prone supported, the prone unsupported, and the kneeling. Both prone positions require you to fire while lying flat on your stomach. The only difference between the two is that the supported position allows—but does not require—you to use sandbags to stabilize your rifle's barrel. We shot at twenty targets from the prone supported, ten from the prone unsupported, and ten from the kneeling position.

On Thursday afternoon, we started qualifications. We each had two chances to qualify that day, and a little more than half the class succeeded. On Friday, those who did not went back to the range to try again. Those who did spent Friday morning in the barracks cleaning weapons.

(While cleaning the weapons is necessary to maintain them properly, the amount of time you will spend cleaning them over the last few weeks will be excessive. The cadre tends to use weapons cleaning as a time filler. After all, you can only wipe down a barrel so many times before it's as clean as it's ever going to be.)

In the afternoon, those who had qualified the day before attended another basic resiliency training course. Friday was a very slow day for those who qualified on Thursday but fairly busy for those who did not. Several people were able to qualify on Friday, but, by the end of DCC, between ten and fifteen percent of the class failed to qualify at all and so did not graduate. As with other graduation requirements, they were given one year to satisfy this requirement with their home units.

While learning to fire an M16 was more difficult for some than for others, if you pay attention to the instruction of the cadre, you'll probably do just fine. While we had several people in our class who had never fired a gun before in their lives, people who had been shooting for decades did not necessarily fare much better. It takes time to adjust to the way the Army wants things done and to firing with your face in the dirt and armor swallowing your body. As an example, I shot the best from the kneeling position—despite its being the most unstable—because it is so similar to how I've been shooting my entire life.

So, if you're experienced with firearms, it's important not to rely too heavily on your past experience. Army training is not the place for arrogance. You should listen to the cadre, even if it is different than what you have done before. Unless you have prior military experience, you probably are not practiced in shooting an assault rifle while lying flat on the ground and wearing thirty pounds of body armor, a utility vest, and a Kevlar helmet.

At the same time, you need to find what is comfortable for you. For example, the Army allows you to use sandbags to stabilize your barrel from the prone supported position. I struggled to shoot well with them, and one of our instructors who was a former sniper hated them. (His antipathy was geared more toward their lack of utility in real-world scenarios, often remarking that he never had a sandbag fall from the sky while engaging in a firefight with the Taliban.) Another member of the cadre, however, loved them and encouraged us all to use them. Personally, I struggled in the beginning, but as soon as I got rid of the sandbags, I easily qualified. Different people have different preferences, and little things like this can make a big difference.

Other Activities

We had only three other notable events during week four. The first was the diagnostic APFT we conducted Monday morning. Since it was not a record test, our scores didn't matter, but it did give us a good idea of how we would perform on the actual test the following Monday.

Everyone must pass the PFT to graduate, so it is an important part of the course.

The second was a four-mile ruck march. Both the four-mile and six-mile ruck marches are graduation requirements.

The final notable event was a visit from the Judge Advocate General of the Army. She came to speak with us for about twenty minutes while we were out at the firing range. We would have many opportunities to see her during the Judge Advocate Officer Basic Course, but with all the traditional Army activities in which we had been engaged over the last several weeks of DCC, it was nice to have a brief connection with the legal profession.

Quick Tips

• Listen to the cadre. The way you have done things in the past is likely not the "Army way."
• While keeping the cadre's instruction in mind, find what is comfortable for you. You will not shoot well if you are uncomfortable. This is a fine line to walk.

DCC: WEEK 5

The fifth week of DCC is the final week with scheduled training events. Week six is devoted to out-processing, the various tasks that must be performed prior to departing Fort Benning—such as cleaning the barracks—and graduation. So while the fifth week is fairly busy, it does mark a noticeable slowdown in the pace of training as the course moves through the final graduation requirements.

Convoy Operations

The first three days of the week were devoted to convoy operations. On Monday, we spent time in the classroom discussing how the Army transports people and supplies by ground in a combat zone. (Air transport procedures were not discussed.)

This class will instruct you in the various lessons that the Army has learned over more than a decade of war. The Army's standard operating procedures and general method of approaching convoy operations have changed significantly since 2001, so this class provides you with the opportunity to learn the latest in Army methodology. It also provides you with the opportunity to learn about what our combat soldiers face and may in fact prepare you for a future mission. It is not unusual for judge advocates to hitch rides on convoys, so this is a very enlightening and important part of training. Driving the point home was a video of an improvised explosive device (IED) explosion a member of our cadre survived in Iraq.

Later in the week, our class traveled across post to the convoy operations simulator. There we were divided into five-man teams with each team being placed into a mock Humvee surrounded by large television screens. The screens were expansive enough that we felt like we were moving when we "drove" the vehicle. In a lot of ways, it reminded me of watching an IMAX movie.

To complete the experience, we were each given a weapon to fire at enemies appearing on the screen. Most of us received M16s or M4s that recoiled as we fired them, though one person operated a 50-caliber machine gun mounted on top of the vehicle. Other than the rudimentary graphics on the screen, the simulator felt surprisingly real.

Through the course of the simulation, we encountered various obstacles, including IEDs and insurgent attacks. When insurgents attacked, my job was to jump out of the vehicle and return fire, but we each had different responsibilities. Overall, it was a lot of fun, though an IED did blow up my vehicle, killing my entire team.

Other Week 5 Tasks

On Monday afternoon, my class tackled the obstacle course. This is one of the stereotypical military training activities, and it is also one of the most enjoyable. There are a lot of interesting obstacles, many of which have to be negotiated at significant heights. It's hard not to laugh as you climb over an obstacle fifty feet in the air and see that the cadre has put down a thin blue gym mat to catch you if you fall. Still, the obstacle course is a lot of fun, if not particularly safe.

On Tuesday and Wednesday, our class divided into two groups, with one group going to the convoy operations simulator I discussed above and the other undergoing MOUT training. (We then switched off the next day.) MOUT, or Military Operations in Urban Terrain, is the Army's method of conducting infantry operations in an urban environment. You can see this in practice in news footage of soldiers breaking down doors in Baghdad. Our instructor was an Army sniper and infantry NCO—and the same instructor who had survived the IED attack—so we were fortunate enough to have an experienced teacher who had actually conducted these operations in a real combat environment.

The rest of the fifth week was devoted to fulfilling the various other graduation requirements. On Monday, we conducted our record APFT. Those who failed had one more chance in week six, and by the end of DCC, only a handful were unable to pass. For judge advocates, however, failing the PFT is not as big a deal as failing the other events. Physical training at the JAG School is pretty intense, and so you'll have plenty of opportunity to pass it in Charlottesville.

We also conducted our six-mile ruck march this week. We had to complete it at a pace no slower than eighteen minutes per mile, and the cadre drove a truck at the minimum speed to help set the pace. While this is not extremely difficult—everyone passed—it is not an incredibly fun experience. The weight of the equipment and the general discomfort of combat boots made this event more difficult than I expected, but, in my opinion, it's not physically challenging; it's just uncomfortable.

On Friday, those who had still failed to qualify on their M16s went back out to the range to try again. The rest of us, however, continued to clean our weapons.

Combat Water Survival

Combat Water Survival Training requires you to complete three events in a large pool, all in full ACUs, including combat boots. The first event requires you to swim fifteen meters while keeping a dummy M16 above the water. The second event requires you to jump off a high dive blindfolded while holding your weapon and then swim back to the edge of the pool with your M16 still in hand. The third event requires you to jump into the water and remove your fighting load carrier, or FLC—pronounced "flick"—underwater before resurfacing. (The FLC is a vest in which you store your combat equipment, such as grenades and magazines.) If you don't panic in the water, you should do fine.

Summary of Week 5

If you pass the requirements on your first attempt, you will have qualified for graduation by the end of the fifth week. The cadre try to use the remaining time in the course to give those who have not yet satisfied the graduation requirements another chance.

The end of this week is an exciting time. As graduation draws nearer and the last of the graduation requirements are fulfilled, you can feel the course coming to a close. You'll find yourself looking forward to moving onto Charlottesville. Once week five comes to an end, you shift from training to be an officer to performing administrative and practical tasks to prepare to leave. By the end of this week, you will feel a sense of accomplishment and pride that comes from successfully completing the challenges of the course. This is an exciting time indeed.

Quick Tips

• While some of the training may not seem pertinent to being a JAG, take the opportunity to learn about the challenges your future clients face in their field.
• Don't panic in the water, and the Combat Water Survival Training should not give you any trouble.

DCC: WEEK 6

Week six marks the end of your time at Fort Benning and the end of the first phase of training. This week is devoted to wrapping up the course and preparing for your departure and the next phase of training. If you are a judge advocate, you will be preparing to make your way to the Judge Advocate Officer Basic Course in Charlottesville, Virginia; if not, you are likely preparing to go home. Consequently, few noteworthy events occur during this week.

Travel During DCC

During my time at DCC, Monday of week six was Presidents Day, so we had a three-day weekend. I used the extra break to travel to Jekyll Island on Georgia's coast. Other than CQ responsibilities, your weekends during DCC will generally be free. This will provide you with the opportunity to travel. Many of my classmates took advantage of this time off to take mini-vacations. Some traveled to Atlanta, others to the beach, and some even flew home. One of my classmates liked to rent a room at a nearby hotel, so that he could watch television and sleep in a real bed. (The beds in the barracks are made of some kind of plastic material, and you can hear the air escape as you sink into them at night.)

There is a limit to how far you can travel by car—usually between two hundred and three hundred miles, depending on whether it is a two or three-day weekend—but you can go anywhere in the continental United States if you travel by air. Of course, you have to get approval to travel, but as long as you stay within the prescribed distance limits, it's generally just a matter of filling out the paperwork.

Wrapping It Up

When we started up again on Tuesday, we returned all of our issued gear to CIF. We then spent the rest of the day—once again—cleaning our weapons. On Tuesday, however, we finally turned them in for good. Of course, after spending a ridiculous amount of time cleaning weapons, you can expect to have the cadre over your shoulder shouting at you to hurry up the last hour or so of cleaning. It's all part of the game. Once you finally get to turn those weapons in for good, it's quite a satisfying feeling.

On Wednesday, we started barracks maintenance. The cadre conducted inspections later in the week, so we had to ensure the barracks were completely clean before we could leave Fort Benning. Also on Wednesday, the cadre from the JAG School in Charlottesville came down to speak with us about our transition from DCC to JAOBC. (If you are not a judge advocate, you can expect to sit through a few briefings completely inapplicable to you.)

We spent Thursday morning wrapping up the last necessary administrative tasks—mostly cleaning, packing, and completing a mountain of paperwork—that were required before leaving Fort Benning. We then spent Thursday afternoon rehearsing for graduation. This is a time-consuming and tedious task. You will practice standing up correctly for what seems like an eternity, but eventually the cadre will consider you acceptable for public presentation and release you for the day. (You may also want to learn the Army Song before showing up.)

Thursday night, we had a social event with the local JAG office at the Fort Benning Brew Pub. The Brew Pub is a popular hangout spot on post, so you will likely become quite familiar with it prior to this event. (Friday night karaoke is particularly popular.) The beer is a selection of microbrews and is mediocre at best, but it's a fun place to hang out with other soldiers.

If you have fulfilled all your graduation requirements, week six will be a long, slow week, as there is very little to do and a lot of waiting around. If you have not, however, the week may be a busy one for you, as the cadre will try to provide you with one last opportunity to graduate.

Graduation

On Friday, graduation finally arrived. The ceremony was a low key event with the post's staff judge advocate—that is Fort Benning's most senior judge advocate, a full-bird colonel—making a few brief remarks and then presenting us with our diplomas. Those who did not graduate did not participate in the ceremony.

After graduation, we were released to travel to Charlottesville, Virginia to begin JAOBC. It's about a ten-hour drive from Fort Benning, Georgia to the Judge Advocate General's Legal Center and School on the campus of the University of Virginia. We were given from 1200 on Friday until 1800 on Saturday to make it to Charlottesville. Some people stayed in a hotel on Friday night, but others made the drive straight through. (I did the latter and wouldn't recommend it.) A few flew.

After six weeks of learning how to be a solider and an officer in the United States Army, you will finally have the opportunity to transition to an academic environment where you will learn to be an Army lawyer. The change in environment is extreme. You will be assigned your own room with hotel-quality accommodations, and you will be staying on the campus of one of the nation's most elite universities. Indeed, the JAG School itself is located right next door to one of the best law schools in the country.

DCC is a good experience, and you should enjoy your time there. You will likely look back on this time fondly and be proud of what you accomplished. Still, while DCC was overall a good experience, few people were sad to see Fort Benning in their rearview mirrors.

Quick Tips

• Keep up with your equipment and keep it in good shape. If it's not clean and dry when you get to CIF, they will not accept it.
• Take advantage of your downtime to travel. If you don't travel, however, you should be able to make advantageous trades of CQ shifts with those who do.

DCC: FINAL THOUGHTS

In the preceding pages, I have provided a brief description of my experiences during DCC, and you should now know what to expect. In this chapter, I want to step back and provide a big-picture view of the Army's Direct Commission Course, offering some of my final thoughts on the training and describing my general impressions of the course as a whole. These are simply my own personal opinions; some of my classmates may not agree with these assessments.

The "City" of Fort Benning

As an exceptionally large post, Fort Benning is like a small city with all the accompanying amenities, including grocery stores, shopping centers, restaurants, and bars. You can find everything you need without ever leaving post.

I discovered, however, that the level of customer service and accessibility that we take for granted in the civilian world is often absent on post. Stores and restaurants close at early hours, often making it difficult to enjoy their services and purchase their products. For example, Clothing and Sales—where you purchase your uniforms—closes at 1800 on weekdays, and the Starbucks on post keeps very weird hours, closing at 1500 on weekends. (I understand it is a bit absurd to complain about the lack of Starbucks while in military training; my point is simply to point out the oddity of the service provided, as most of those taking advantage of the amenities on post are not in training.)

The quality of service is not always up to civilian standards, either. That is not to say that the people are rude; I did not find that to be the case at all. They simply do not have access to the tools necessary to provide good service. As a way of illustration, when I purchased my service uniform from Clothing and Sales, I also purchased the accompanying nameplates. Three weeks later, the nameplates had not yet arrived—in fact, they did not come in until after I had left Fort Benning—so I went to Ranger Joe's right off post. (The fact that there is a place off post that is able to compete successfully with on-post facilities despite having to charge sales tax is telling in and of itself.) I watched as the clerk made the nameplates right in front of me. What Clothing and Sales could not accomplish in three weeks, Ranger Joe's accomplished in thirty seconds.

Many local businesses have done very well for themselves by offering the same services available on post with a manner of business efficiency and customer service lacking in the military. Prices, however, are often significantly better on post, so it's a tradeoff.

After spending time in the Army, I suspect that the military vote tends to lean Republican because of the ubiquity of government in military life. The inefficiency, byzantine bureaucratic structures, and invasive government authority defines life in the military, and many service members—even those like me who love the military—are skeptical of efforts to expand this model into larger society. (Of course, no opinion is universal, and I understand many would likely disagree with this overly-simplistic assessment.)

Another interesting note is that Fort Benning is an open post. Having grown up on military bases where everyone needed a military ID—and, at that time, stickers on their car—to get on post, this came as a surprise to me. Anyone with a driver's license can get onto Fort Benning.

Consequently, you have to be careful on post and be mindful of your own safety, just as you would anywhere else. While it is safe, you cannot relax as if you were in a completely secure environment. While I was at DCC, for example, our cadre had to run off squatters they discovered in our barracks. You should therefore not allow the fact that you are on a military post to lull you into a false sense of security.

The Civilians

During your time at DCC, you will likely encounter civilian personnel performing administrative functions on post. Much of the paperwork required to receive your pay, benefits, reimbursements, and a variety of other needs will be handled and processed by these civilians. I don't think it's hyperbole to say that you will likely find these people to be some of the most rude, incompetent, and generally unpleasant people that you will encounter in the military. The Army outsources much of its administrative work to civilians, and the result is a cohort of disrespectful and apathetic bureaucratic functionaries on whom you must rely for your livelihood. (It is telling that there is a large sign hanging on the wall at CIF reminding the civilian workers that they should not view soldiers as an inconvenience.)

A few people in my class did not receive paychecks for weeks, and almost all of the prior service officers were consistently underpaid. Dealing with these civilians can be very frustrating and taxing, and it is unfair that those answering the call to service are treated so poorly by those hired to take care of them.

(I should note that these civilians should not be confused with the higher-level civilians working elsewhere in the Army. I generally found these civilians to be very competent and professional.)

The only reason I use such strong language is to prepare you to address this issue appropriately and not become disillusioned with the Army on account of this one unfavorable aspect of military life. Every job has its unpleasant facets, and so you should not allow difficult civilians to tarnish your view of the Army or make you regret your decision to serve.

My only advice is to be ready for this and try to be patient and maintain a good attitude. Be very polite to the civilians. It's hard enough to get them to do what they are supposed to do for you; if you make them angry, it will be nearly impossible. This is not the private sector where you can complain to the manager to increase your chances of good service. There seems to be very little accountability, so appealing to a higher authority will likely get you nowhere. Remember that, no matter how they treat you, you are still an officer in the United States Army and must conduct yourself as such, setting an example of maturity and etiquette. Just be persistent.

As way of illustration of the type of thing you may have to address, I will share one of my own experiences—an experience quite benign compared to those of my classmates. When we first arrived, I completed two forms to receive my uniform allowance, which was about $650—well short of what uniforms actually cost but significant nonetheless. The civilian taking these forms lost one of mine. (Whenever they lose something, it means you didn't submit it. Just roll with it as it's not a point worth arguing.) She still had one of the forms, however, which means that she knew my name, unit, and contact information, but instead of contacting me and letting me know she needed more information to ensure I was paid, she just filed it away and did nothing. She waited until I contacted her after my allowance was a month late, and, had I never contacted her, I would have never received this allowance. You have to follow up constantly to ensure these civilians do their jobs. You need to be prepared for this and accept that this is the status quo.

Of course, while this is the general reputation of the civilian administrators, you will find a significant number who love soldiers and take pride in their work. Their reputations suffer unfairly on account of the ineptitude of others, but to you they will seem like a glass of cool water in a bureaucratic desert. If you run into one of these great civilians, do whatever you can for them. Thank them profusely, write a letter to their supervisor, and sing their praises wherever you can. They work in a culture of complacency and yet come to work every day to serve you. Make your gratitude known.

Passing the Course

If you put forth your best effort and have a good attitude, you will probably find that the class is not that challenging. While we had a handful of people fail to graduate, almost all of them failed to qualify on their weapons. Your chances of qualifying at your home unit are likely to be much better, so, while you obviously want to qualify at DCC if you can, don't sweat it too much if you can't.

The other graduation requirements are the ruck marches, the APFT, and land navigation. They aren't a lot of fun—except land navigation, assuming the weather cooperates—but they also are not difficult to complete. As I stated earlier, only a handful of my classmates failed the APFT, so as long as you show up in somewhat decent shape, you should be fine. Remedial PT will be conducted at Charlottesville, so everyone should pass by the time JAG training is complete. (If you are not a judge advocate, however, I would make sure to show up in great shape.) None of the other graduation requirements gave anyone any real trouble.

Attitude

The Army—and the military in general—is notorious for its "hurry up and wait" philosophy. Essentially, you will rush to get things done and get somewhere by a certain time, only to then wait around doing nothing for several hours. Realize that you are in the Army and this is part of it.

This waiting applies to almost everything. When you qualify with your rifle, for example, you will spend all but maybe forty-five minutes of a twelve-hour day waiting around for your turn to shoot. There are a lot of people who need a chance to do one particular activity, so this is just the nature of the beast. Embrace it and keep a good attitude. ("Embrace the suck" is a phrase with which you will become quite familiar and that I would recommend taking to heart.) Attitude is key.

Think of DCC like a baseball game. The vast majority of your time is spent waiting around for something to happen; when something actually does happen, however, it's usually pretty cool. Understand this going in, and you'll be more likely to enjoy yourself.

Concluding Thoughts

So, in closing, I would simply say that DCC is not that difficult. Anyone with a good attitude who puts forth a good effort should be successful. There will inevitably be things that frustrate you about the course, but you should just take it all in stride. If you think something is stupid, just do it without complaining—safety issues and potentially illegal activities being the notable exceptions. About half of these seemingly stupid things will actually make pretty good sense after you learn the reasoning behind them; the other half will still seem stupid.

Realize that your opinion usually doesn't matter. Don't develop a reputation as the soldier who constantly complains. By choosing to join the JAG Corps, you have chosen to put up with some of the tedious requirements of military life. Believe me, it's well worth it.

DCC was a good experience for me, and I'm grateful to have had the opportunity to attend. I understand that some people interested in the military are nervous about the initial training requirements, whether that be basic training, officer candidate school, or DCC. If you are a direct commission officer, however, you shouldn't be. The cadre wants you to succeed; DCC is not a screening process designed to weed people out of the Army. If you put forth the effort and take it seriously—without taking yourself too seriously—you should be successful.

Quick Tips

- Always keep a good attitude. You are an officer in the United States Army and set the example for other soldiers.
- Put forth your best effort, and you will do fine!

CONCLUSION

I appreciate your purchasing my book, and I hope that you've found it valuable. I will continue my description of the Army's initial JAG training in my forthcoming book *The JAG School Survival Guide*.

If you have any questions or comments that you would like to share, or if there is any additional information you would like included in future editions of this book, please feel free to contact me directly at garrett@garrettham.com. I would be particularly interested to hear about any changes to the program that have occurred since I graduated DCC in February 2014.

If you enjoyed this book and would like to be notified when I release future books, including my forthcoming *The JAG School Survival Guide*, you can sign up for my mailing list at www.garrettham.com/sign-up. You can also follow me on Twitter @garrettham_esq. I wish you luck as you pursue your goal of becoming an Army JAG officer.

ABOUT THE AUTHOR

Garrett Ham is an alumnus of both Ouachita Baptist University and the University of Arkansas School of Law, graduating *summa cum laude* from both institutions. Garrett currently resides with his wife and two children in northwest Arkansas, where he works as an attorney and serves as an officer and judge advocate in the United States Army National Guard. Additional information about Garrett and his writings can be found at www.garrettham.com.

Made in the USA
San Bernardino, CA
06 April 2019